CW00738946

Compiled by Jocelyn Lukins and Christopher Evans

Especial thanks to:

Bonhams who allowed me to photograph their star figures through the years.

The Whitley Collection for their friendship, enthusiasm and help.

Royal Doulton and their artists for producing the most exciting figurine range ever.

Cover photograph of Rhythm HN1903 by Jason Fraser

Graphic design and layout by Jean Goodwin

Published by Venta books

Printed and bound in Great Britain by J. Thomson Colour Printers, Glasgow

ISBN 978 - 0 - 9510288 - 9 - 6

Ventafile

The majority of photographs and illustrations in this book have been supplied by Ventafile, a compilation of materials and information assembled by Jocelyn Lukins.

A Doulton catalogue page 1914

In the mid 1970s Royal Doulton realised that a record of their HN figure productions was needed for the collector. Paul Atterbury, then Historical Officer for Royal Doulton, was appointed editor and the landmark volume was begun. Any pattern books which still existed and any figurines were retrieved from the obscurity of factory corners and the task of listing the 2000 figures was begun. There were almost no figurines found at the factory so that Richard Dennis, dealing from his shop in Kensington Church Street, was called upon to supply one of each model from HN1. The search didn't prove easy and it soon became worldwide. The United States, where most collectors were located, was a good source but so were the auction rooms as far afield as New Zealand for instance. As the collection grew, Paul Atterbury asked me to research the backgrounds of the titles. I didn't realise at the time that it would turn into a life interest. History had been my best subject at school but I never realised that the hours I spent in the attic pouring over piles of *Film Weekly* and *Picturegoer, Woman and Home* and *Everywoman* magazines from the 1920s and 30s or my love of the theatre and cinema would ever have such value.

The research took over six months but although it was published in 1978 things didn't stop there and haven't yet and I've said many times that this record might be published posthumously. However in meeting with Christopher Evans, who has the same passion and enthusiasm for the subject, has given the project the required impetus to present this selection at last; just a taste of some of the influences. JL

Royal Doulton Figures, the ultimate reference book, was first published 1978 with further editions 1987 and 1994.

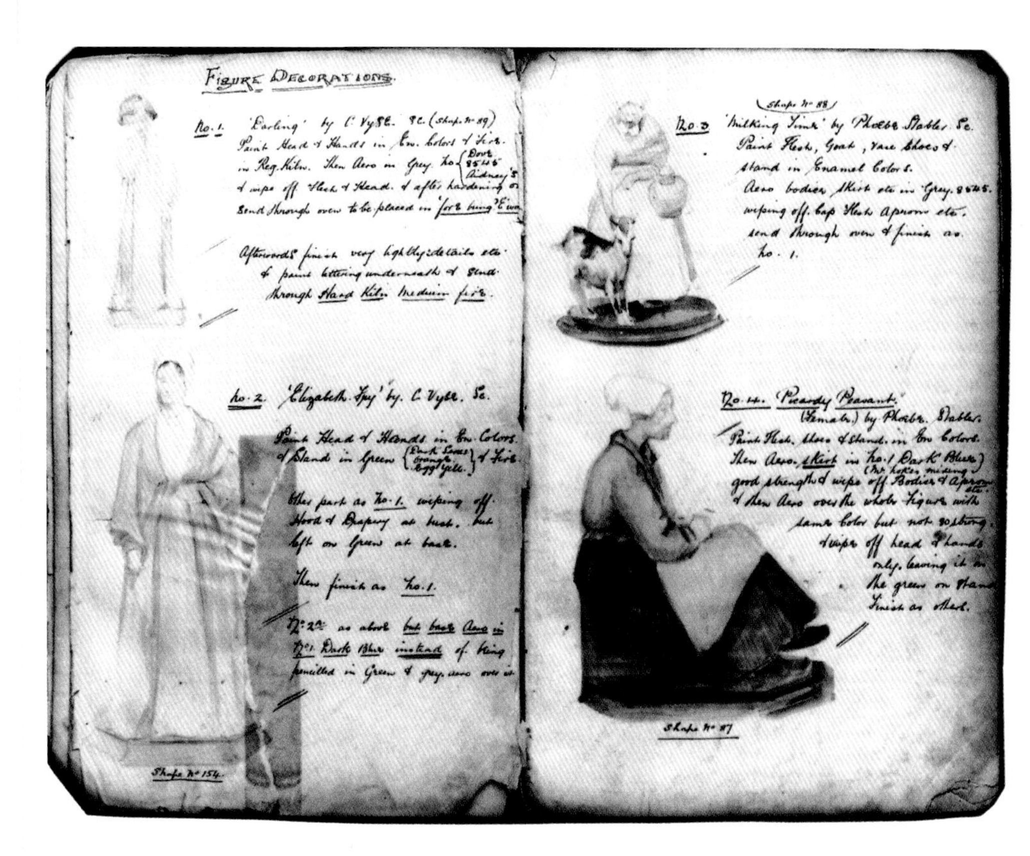

Figure Decorations.

No. 1. 'Darling' by C. Vyse. Sc. (Shape No 89)
Paint Head & Hands in En. Colors & fire
in Reg. Kiln. Then Aero in Grey No (Dove 8545 Aidney's)
& wipe off Flesh & Head. & after hardening on
send through oven to be placed in 'fire bung' E [illegible]

Afterwards finish very lightly details etc.
& paint lettering underneath & send
through Hard Kiln Medium fire.

Shape No 154.

No. 2. 'Elizabeth Fry' by C. Vyse. Sc.

Paint Head & Hands in En. Colors
& Stand in Green (Dark Lemon, Orange, Egg yell.) & fire.

Other part as No. 1. wiping off
Hood & Drapery at back. but
left on Green at back.

Then finish as No. 1.

No. 2a as above but back Aero in
No. 1 Dark Blue instead of being
pencilled in Green & grey. [illegible]

(Shape No 88)
No. 3 'Milking Time' by Phoebe Stabler Sc.
Paint Flesh, Goat, Vase Shoes &
Stand in Enamel Colors.
Aero bodice, Skirt etc in Grey. 8545.
wiping off. Cap Flesh Apron etc.
send through oven & finish as
No. 1.

No. 4. "Picardy Peasant."
(Female.) by Phoebe Stabler.
Paint Flesh, Shoes & Stand in En colors.
Then Aero. Skirt in No. 1 Dark Blue)
(Mr [illegible] mixing)
good strength & wipe off Bodice & Apron etc.
& then Aero over the whole figure with
same color but not so strong.
& wipe off head & hands
only, leaving it on
the green on Stand
Finish as other.

Shape No 87

THE ROYAL DOULTON FIGURE PATTERN BOOKS

VALERIE BAYNTON

In the Doulton Archives the pattern books showing the figures range are some of the most interesting. They were generally maintained by one person whose responsibility it was to draw each design into the books, colour it accurately and add any special manufacturing or decorating instructions such as a specific type of body or glaze. When a repeat order was received the appropriate page in the design book was consulted and using this, and perhaps also a finished example or pattern as a guide, the artist could reproduce the desired effect. Despite being used for such a mundane but essential purpose, the pattern books are literally works of art, with original paintings illustrating the colours and decorating techniques used for each figure. Sadly the men or women who actually kept the design books are unknown.

The figure design books are particularly important because several colour variations can exist for the same figure, but each variation has a unique HN number and generally an entry in the HN pattern books to record it. For example, HN 402 and HN 403 are both variations of the figure Betty.

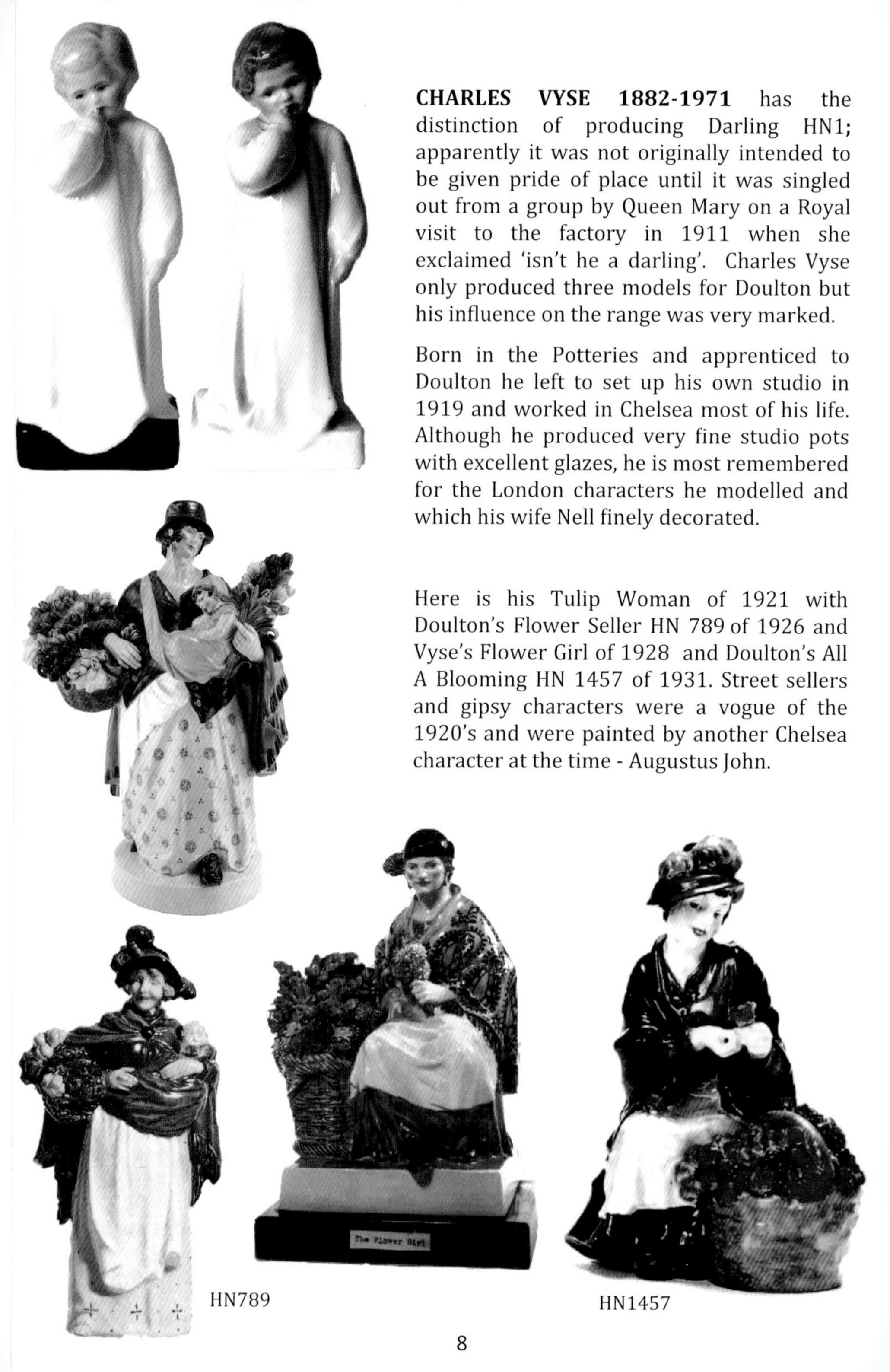

CHARLES VYSE 1882-1971 has the distinction of producing Darling HN1; apparently it was not originally intended to be given pride of place until it was singled out from a group by Queen Mary on a Royal visit to the factory in 1911 when she exclaimed 'isn't he a darling'. Charles Vyse only produced three models for Doulton but his influence on the range was very marked.

Born in the Potteries and apprenticed to Doulton he left to set up his own studio in 1919 and worked in Chelsea most of his life. Although he produced very fine studio pots with excellent glazes, he is most remembered for the London characters he modelled and which his wife Nell finely decorated.

Here is his Tulip Woman of 1921 with Doulton's Flower Seller HN 789 of 1926 and Vyse's Flower Girl of 1928 and Doulton's All A Blooming HN 1457 of 1931. Street sellers and gipsy characters were a vogue of the 1920's and were painted by another Chelsea character at the time - Augustus John.

HN789

HN1457

ELIZABETH FRY HN 2 1913 Charles Vyse

A Quaker prison reformer, 1780 - 1845 who worked for the improvement of the conditions of women prisoners and who, with her brother John Gurney, issued an influential report on prison reform in 1819.

This model was copied from a statue by Drury which stands outside the Central Criminal Court at the Old Bailey, London. I needed a police escort to view the original. A prison reformer to decorate your sitting room? Noke didn't get this right and consequently this is a very rare figure.

GAINSBOROUGH HAT HN 675 1924 Harry Tittensor

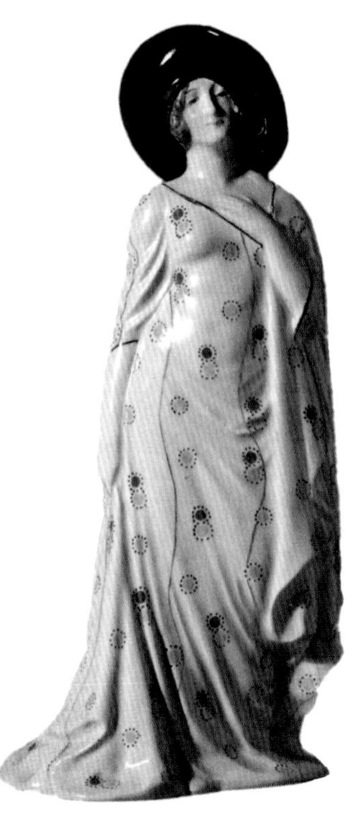

One would have expected this figure to have been a direct copy of a particular Gainsborough painting - perhaps his portrait of the Duchess of Devonshire - but it was the hats which many of his sitters wore which influenced the title. The reference here is much less direct than in other historical images.

Tittensor was a local art master, a versatile, all-round artist who played an important part in setting up the figurines department for Charles Noke.

THE LAND OF NOD HN 56 1916 Harry Tittensor

UPON HER CHEEKS SHE WEPT HN 59 1916 Laurence Perugini

A CHILD'S GRACE HN 62 1916 Laurence Perugini

Three years into the range Charles Noke must have realised that with the popularity of Darling HN 1, in production for forty years, over Elisabeth Fry HN 2, that child studies were desirable. A group of these were commissioned based on children's poems. The Land Of Nod HN 56 came from *A Child's Garden of Verses* by Robert Stevenson, published in 1885. It showed a small boy going to bed with his candle and on the base was painted *Every night I go abroad / Afar into the Land of Nod.*

Another similar figure, Upon Her Cheeks She Wept HN 59, was modelled by Perugini, Charles Dicken's son-in-law. The title was taken from a poem *Upon Electra's Tears* by Robert Herrick.

Perugini also did Shy Anne HN 60 from a poem by A A Milne and A Child's Grace HN62 from *Another Grace* by Herrick. Harry Tittensor added to the series with The Little Land HN 63 from a poem of the same name by Robert Stevenson. All these were modelled in 1916 with some lines from the poems painted on the plinths.

These figures repeated the theme of HN 1 but not its long run. Between 1914 and 1917, 148 of Darling were sold as opposed to only 7 of The Little Land.

PHOEBE STABLER

Another figure modeller of that time was Phoebe Stabler who worked at their Hammersmith studio with her sculptor husband Harold. An astute woman, she cashed in on her designs a little more by selling the licence to reproduce them to four different potteries.

Here is her Lavender Woman HN 22 of 1913 and her Flower Girl for Worcester of 1931.

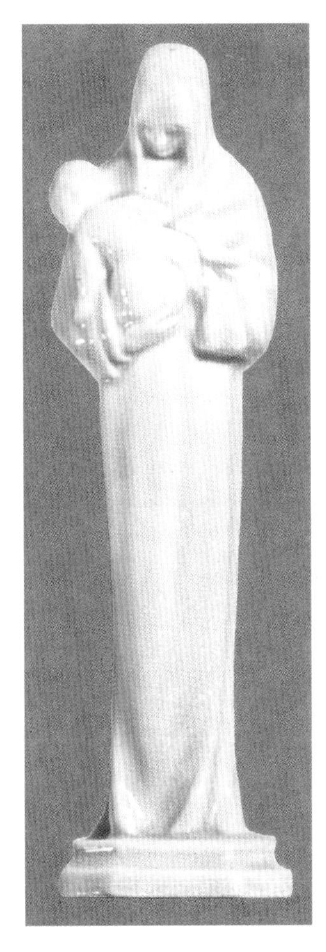

Sleep HN 24, which she had produced for Doulton in 1913, became a Madonna for the Ashtead pottery who employed disabled ex-servicemen from the First World War.

In these cases the Doulton figures were produced first but, with Picardy Peasants HN 4 & 5 of 1913, the same models were made by the Poole pottery in 1910.

Phoebe Stabler did seven successful figures for Doulton but her Milking Time HN 3 had little appeal and sold badly. This also became The Old Goat Woman for Worcester. These were experimental times.

The most successful was Madonna of the Square HN 10 which was made in 14 different colours through the years from 1913, the last being HN 2034 in 1949.

In 2010 this lavender colourway achieved £1050 at auction, whereas the blue version by Poole made only £240 in the same sale; clearly showing the premium on Doulton figures. The square referred to was Sloane Square, Chelsea. Charles Vyse did a much more colourful flower seller with that title.

EUROPA & THE BULL HN 95
1918 Ernest Light

Here the style of the Stablers' model was copied by Ernest Light for Doulton.

Light was an art teacher in the Potteries who exhibited at the Royal Society of Artists in Birmingham.

Children on a Bull by
Harold and Phoebe Stabler
for Poole Pottery

ELLEN TERRY & HENRY IRVING

Charles Noke's early *Vellum* figures of the 1880's and 90's were mainly theatrical subjects and many of these featured the most popular actors of their times, Henry Irving and Ellen Terry. Irving was the actor manager of the Lyceum Theatre in London from 1878 - 1902 and his leading lady was Ellen Terry. Irving was responsible for reviving the popular interest in Shakespeare. He overcame a stammer to become a great actor and was the first to be knighted. In 1919 Noke adapted some of his early *Vellum* figures for the HN range, including one of Irving in *Henry VIII* in his role as Cardinal Wolsey HN 344 and Ellen Terry as Queen Catherine HN 379. The costumes were very authentic and at 13", the figures were large. In 1925 Noke adapted his Mephistopheles and Marguerite HN 755 from Goethe's *Faust.* At 7", it was more in line with current figures. As with his *Vellum* original this was a double sided Janus figure.

Irving and Terry's partnership lasted for 24 years and was referred to as one 'of the glories of the London stage' but they in fact toured the whole of England and North America in their roles in *Henry VIII, Romeo and Juliet, The Merchant of Venice* and *Faust.* Noke captured Irving's ascetic features in his early model. Ellen Terry said of him, 'He was quiet, patient, tolerant, impersonal, gentle, close, crafty and incapable of caring for anything outside his work'. I feel Charles Noke and Henry Irving were similar types in their brilliance and dedication to their work and perhaps a little dull, quite unlike Ellen Terry who came from a theatrical family and made her first appearance on the stage at the age of nine. At the end of her career she appeared at a benefit performance in 1906 with 22 actor members of her family; her great nephew was Sir John Gielgud. She married three times, first to the artist G. F. Watts, she a beauty of 17 and he 30 years her senior. She left him and formed a liaison with the talented architect and designer E. W. Godwin. They became the

centre of a brilliant social circle which included Oscar Wilde and Bernard Shaw. Watts had delayed an annulment so that they couldn't marry but she had two children with him, a boy, Edward Gordon Craig, who became a theatrical designer and a daughter, Edith, who became an actress. She then returned to the stage and later married two of her leading men. With the second of these, James Carew an American, she toured North America playing Shakespeare. Edith did not approve of this liaison as her stepfather was younger than herself!

Queen Catherine HN379

DORIS KEANE AS CAVALINI

Ellen Terry ended her career lecturing on Shakespeare in North America. In 1925 she was created a Dame, probably never having been socially acceptable before. One of her last Shakespearian roles on the stage was as the nurse in *Romeo and Juliet* in 1919. Juliet was played by an American actress, Doris Keane, and Romeo by a young English actor, Basil Sydney, twelve years her junior, whom she married. Doris Keane was a renowned beauty and is immortalised by Royal Doulton. She rocketed to stardom in her role in *Romance,* which opened in 1913 in the States. It played for two years there and a further four years in London, after which she and Basil Sydney returned to the States and toured in it again. In this popular, rather risqué play, Doris Keane played an Italian opera singer, a dramatic personality, who always wore black and carried a pet monkey. She is loved by a young clergyman from New York and he gives her his mother's pearls and pendant which you see on the figure. She loves him too but has a 'past' and realises this will ruin his career when it is found out, as it concerned his patron. They part, she saying dramatically, 'you are the only man I have ever loved'. She continues as a famous opera singer, he becomes a bishop and they die still loving one another. The tempestuous love scenes, her disrobing onstage and the clergyman hero made this a great popular success on both sides of the Atlantic. When Doris Keane arrived in England by liner she was mobbed. She appeared with the matinee idol Owen Nares and *Romance* ran for over a thousand performances in London alone.

HN 90 & HN 96 1918 Charles Noke 11"

A figurine of Doris Keane was made at Lambeth in 1919. It was modelled by John Broad and made in the special porcelain body invented by Joseph Mott. At Burslem, the figure was later reissued as Rosamund HN 1551 and as a miniature Rosamund M 32, both in 1932.

W S PENLEY AS CHARLEY'S AUNT HN 35
1914 Albert Toft

The contemporary theatre continued to influence Noke's figurine range. W S Penley was popular in his role as *Charley's Aunt,* playing an Oxford undergraduate who impersonates an aunt from Brazil who was to act as a chaperone to some young ladies he and his friends wished to entertain. *Charley's Aunt* by Brandon Thomas ran for 1,466 performances after opening in 1913. A Doulton figurine of the main character was presented to ladies in the audience on the 21st performance on December 21st 1913 at the Prince of Wales Theatre. About 500-600 copies of this figure were commissioned. Other commemorative gifts were given on other special anniversary performances. Early in his career in 1916, Noel Coward played the part of Charley. The play is still popular today with amateur dramatic groups.

The figure was modelled by Albert Toft (1862-1949) who taught Leslie Harradine at Camberwell School of Art at evening classes whilst he was serving his apprenticeship at Doulton Lambeth. Toft himself had studied at Stoke on Trent and later at the Royal College of Art.

LEON BAKST 1866-1924

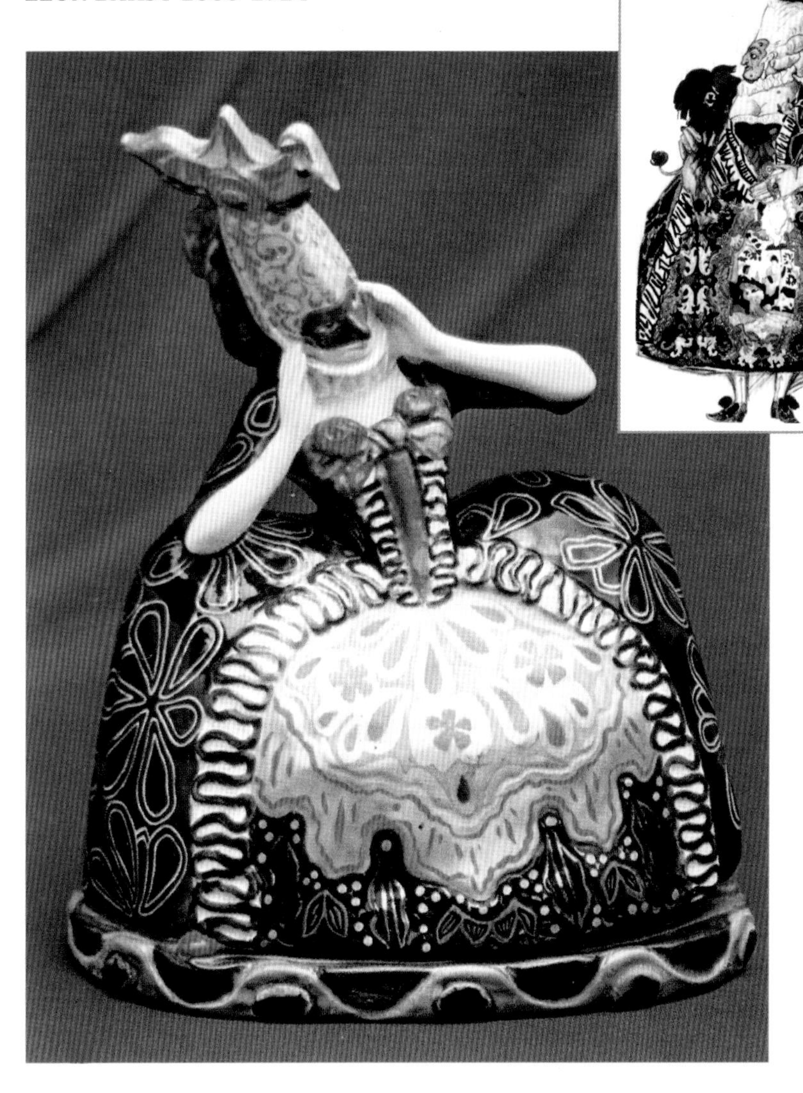

A strong influence on the figurine range at this time was this Russian artist who designed scenery and costumes for Diaghilev's *Ballets Russes.* One design had a very direct connection with one of the ballets. It portrayed the Marquise Sylvestra role in *Les Femmes de Bonne Humeur* at Rome in 1917. It could have been a special commission or prototype as only two copies have been found to date. The Bakst influence was mainly seen in the decoration of figurines in the current range where Bakst's practice of making costumes from many contrasting textile designs was copied.

The Bakst treatment was given to The Princess HN 392 , The Necklace HN 394 (formally called Lady Without Bouquet), Contentment HN 395, The Bouquet HN 406, Lady With A Shawl HN 447, Fruit Gathering HN 562, The Curtsey HN 670 and Tulips HN 747.

Many more were made between 1920 and 1924, regardless of subject. It was an attractive style but maybe a little avant-garde for the figurine market at the time. They could not have sold in large quantities as they are all rare today.

The Princess HN 392

The Bouquet
HN 406

The Necklace
HN 394

The Curtsey
HN 670

Lady With A Shawl
HN 447

Tulips HN 747

LADY ERMINE HN 54 1916 Charles Noke

The fashions of the time must have influenced these figures.

Lady Ermine was also known as 'Ermine Muff'.

OUT FOR A WALK HN 86
1918 Ernest Light

DANCING FIGURE
HN 311 1927 20"

This figure is a direct copy of a *Lady Musician* made at the French Sèvres factory in 1903 in an edition of 10. It was designed by Agathon Leonard in biscuit porcelain; a copy is in the Chicago Museum of Fine Art. This Doulton version HN 311 is dated 1927 and was found in Australia having been bought on a visit to Nile Street in 1927. It was not put into production, probably due to its vulnerability. It appears in an illustration of a shop display in Australia in the 1920s. Noke was obviously still seeking inspiration in many areas and setting his standards very high.

DIGGER (Australian) HN 353 1919 Ernest Light 11"

The model for this figure was Gunner John Arthur Butler Shorter of the 41st Battalion, Australian Service Corps. In the First World War he served in Egypt and then in the thick of the fighting in Belgium and France where he was gassed. Whilst he was in Europe he visited the Burslem factory where he was well known as a member of the Shorter family of Doulton retailers in Australia. It was he who insisted on this very casual pose with his hands in his pockets. Art director Charles Noke objected that 'sculptural images should have hands' but Gunner Shorter stuck to his guns and the resultant figure embodies the popular conception of the Australian 'Digger' of the First World War. When he returned down-under he left the retailing business and farmed in New South Wales, dying at 92 in 1982.

'Digger' was the name originally given to Australian gold miners in the 19th century but came to be a name given to any ANZAC soldier.

This was one of a set of three infantry men in the First World War. Two represented Australia and New Zealand and the other, entitled *Blighty*, represented the British forces.

They were produced in two glazes, khaki and *Titanian*.

PAVLOVA HN 487 1921

Anna Pavlova, (1882 - 1931) a Russian prima ballerina travelled throughout the world popularising classical ballet. She appeared in music halls as a solo act reaching a very wide public. Her most famous performance was as *The Dying Swan* set to *Le Cygne* by Saint-Saëns and illustrated by this figure. She was very popular in Australia and New Zealand where they created the Pavlova dessert for her.

WILLIAM GILBERT AND ARTHUR SULLIVAN

Yum Yum HN 2899
Bill Harper 1980

The two gentlemen caricatured here had a great influence on the range. The Savoy Operas were produced by Richard D'Oyly Carte who had instigated the partnership and were a great success from their inception. They have become a part of 'Britishness'. The 'perfect professional partnership' thus formed was never easy. Sullivan saw himself as a classical composer; it was he who wrote *The Lost Chord* and the grand opera *Ivanhoe* which he prized above the music he wrote to accompany Gilbert's comic librettos. However the comic operettas are as relevant and popular today as ever, especially on the amateur stage, whereas their other works are rarely performed.

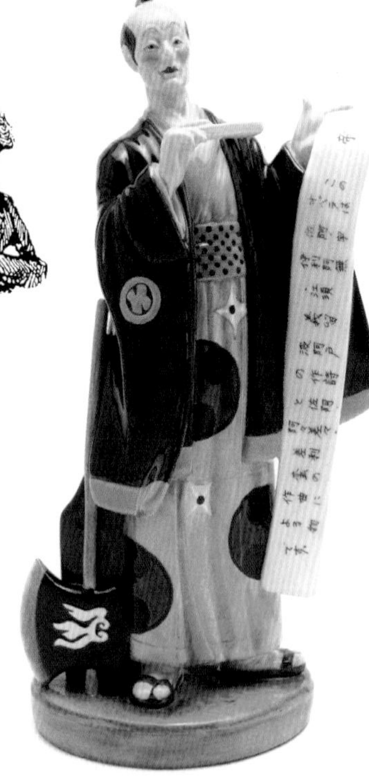

Ko Ko HN 2898
Bill Harper 1980

Doulton issued a host of characters from the operettas from 1924-1993.

HENRY LYTTON AS JACK POINT HN 85 1918 Charles Noke

Jack Point HN 2080

Charles Noke had access to the stage costume belonging to Henry Lytton in the role of Jack Point in Gilbert & Sullivan's *Yeomen of the Guard.* The jester was a favourite subject of Noke's and appears in many colourways and sizes in the range. A larger 16" version, Jack Point HN 2080 modelled by him was in production for over 80 years. Other characters were taken from *The Pirates of Penzance* and *The Mikado.*

Leslie Harradine produced more characters in the 1920s and Bill Harper did a series of six in the 1980s.

THE COBBLER FROM CHU CHIN CHOW HN 542 1922 Charles Noke

THE POTTER HN 1493 1932 Charles Noke

There was a great fascination with the idea of the exotic East in the early 20th century. *Chu Chin Chow,* a musical play, opened in 1916 and ran for 2000 performances in London, the longest run ever until *The Mousetrap.* It was based on the story of *Ali Baba and the 40 Thieves.* My grandmother took me to see it as a very young child and I can't remember being fazed by the cobbler sewing the pieces of a body together! In the London production there was a potter throwing pots in the market place. He was Harry Peacock who played the part on the stage in the evenings after his day throwing at the Doulton Lambeth factory. Charles Noke's Potter HN 1493 was in the range for sixty years. Because of the display of pots the figure was made up of 16 parts each of which was moulded separately. This figure and The Scribe HN324, the Snake Charmer HN 1317 and the Mendicant HN 1355 were all inspired by this fascination with Eastern themes. The silent cinema produced *The Sheik* in 1921 with Rudolf Valentino and there were many following plays and films to popularise the theme. Doulton Burslem decorated many fine *Flambé* vases and issued series ware with desert scenes in the 20s and 30s.

In 1924 John Bailey, sales manager at Burslem, made a sales tour to Australia just as Michael Doulton does today, but Bailey's took much longer and his return was such an occasion that a banquet was held at which Charles Noke's son, Jack, gave his rendering of the cobbler's song from *Chu Chin Chow.* This menu cover records the event.

OMAR KHAYYAM AND THE BELOVED HN 419   1920 Charles Noke

This group and Omar Khayyam HN 408, also modelled by Noke and issued in the same year, continues the European interest in Eastern themes which led to colourful advertisements and this theatre bill.

The Rubaiyat of Omar Khayyam translated from the Persian by Edward Fitzgerald in 1859 expresses the popular sentiment of 'enjoy all that life offers while you may.'

HENRY VIII HN 1792 1933 Charles Noke

Modellers have to take a lot of care in research. Peggy Davies visited art galleries and museums for that purpose and even an abattoir on one occasion. If modellers had a good reference library it was helpful and Christopher Evans has found a volume with coloured illustrations of historical costumes by Dion Clayton Calthrop which was obviously used as a source by at least two of the modellers. Charles Noke took his inspiration for his Henry VIII from a work by Hans Holbein and his Old King HN 358 could have had its origins in the Bayeux Tapestry.

There are many historical characters in the figure range from Christopher Columbus to Sir Winston Churchill and all of them have been carefully researched, it is part of the brief to the modeller. Mistakes can occur when enthusiastic marketing men change things at a later stage, giving John Peel a red coat instead of his grey one for instance because' red sells'.

KING CHARLES HN 404 1920 Charles Noke & Harry Tittensor 16.75"

This figure was copied from a drawing by Bernard Partridge of Henry Irving in his role as King Charles I.

ST GEORGE HN 2067 1950 Stanley Thorogood 16"

This large *Prestige* piece was adapted from an original by Stanley Thorogood exhibited in 1915.

JANICE HN 2165 1955 Peggy Davies

This was copied from a contemporary painting of the 13 year old Princess Elizabeth, later Queen Elizabeth I.

THE VOGUE FOR "DUTCH"

I can understand the fascination with the mysterious East. It was unknown to most people and the colour and exoticism was found in the pages of *The Arabian Nights*, but why was everything 'Dutch' so popular in the first three decades of the twentieth century? Dutch girls featured in a 1901 advert selling Raleigh bicycles and Player's Navy Mixture tobacco in 1904. In the theatre there were musical comedies such as *Miss Hook of Holland* and popular songs like *Tiptoe Through the Tulips.*

At the Burslem factory the most popular and therefore the most prolific design in series-ware was *Harlem* and for Lambeth Leslie Harradine produced a group of Dutch characters and vases. Later the HN range took up the theme and issued Gretchen HN 1397 and Derrick HN 1398 in 1930. Annette HN 1471 in 1931 and Willy-Won't He HN 1561 in 1933.

They were all modelled by Leslie Harradine.

Aged 78. 1961

LESLIE HARRADINE (1887-1965)

This cheerful man was the most brilliant of the Doulton figure designers. He was apprenticed at the Doulton Lambeth factory working under George Tinworth and John Broad from 1902 until 1908 when he left to set up his own studio. However, he continued to work freelance for Doulton Lambeth until he left to farm in Canada with his brother in 1915. In 1916 in the First World War the brothers served in France in Canadian cavalry regiments. Leslie had two horses shot from under him and the second fell on him and injured his leg so that he was hospitalised after only 21 days on active service! After the war Charles Noke tried to persuade Harradine to come to work with him at Burslem. Noke had always admired Charles Dickens and had particularly liked the set of Dickens characters Harradine had modelled for Lambeth. Harradine enjoyed the freedom of his own pottery and refused the offer but arranged to prepare models and send them to Burslem by post. Joseph Mott, Art Director at Lambeth, arranged a single meeting between Noke and Harradine at his London office. From then on for almost forty years Harradine sent eagerly awaited brown paper parcels containing his proposed models to Burslem from Sark in the Channel Islands, Majorca and Spain where he lived. He never visited the Burslem factory.

He made prototypes for the Dickens miniature range introduced in 1922 - there are alternative versions for some of them. He added to this range in 1932 as well as doing six characters in the 7" size. Dickens's characters are always popular.

Harradine married three times and fathered five daughters and a son. His daughter, Helen, from his second marriage told me that her father had definitely married her mother for her beauty rather than her brains. She had been his model and was only 17 when they married. When Harradine left one day with only a suitcase, she managed badly. She had to sell all his models and found it difficult to cope. Helen knew the first Mrs Harradine and also told me, 'all his wives loved him unquestionably to the end'.

Leslie Harradine died in a Gibraltar hospital in 1965. I've heard it had an appropriate Doulton architectural exterior. This lively, very human person lives on in his creations as some of his models were still selling after sixty years. It was he who found the successful formula Charles Noke had searched for.

I discovered which magazines his first wife read, for Harradine used them to find images from the illustrations and advertisements for his models. One of them was an advertisement in *Good Housekeeping* for 'Cyclax' bath salts and was the inspiration for The Bather HN 597 1924. Harradine's models were a true reflection of their time.

THE BEGGAR'S OPERA - JOHN GAY 1728 - Leslie Harradine 1921
POLLY PEACHUM HN 463, CAPTAIN MACHEATH HN 464,
THE BEGGAR HN 526, THE HIGHWAYMAN HN 527, LUCY LOCKETT HN 695

This eighteenth century musical play was revived at the Lyric Theatre, Hammersmith in 1920 and for many years after. The costumes were designed by Claud Lovat Fraser, a brilliant young designer who was the first to bring realism into the theatre. His costumes, once made up, were thrown onto the studio floor and walked upon, had paint thrown on them and where suitable, as with the beggar's costume, slashed He reasoned that as the characters in the play were from London street life of the eighteenth century, some of whom spent a lot of their time in jail, they wouldn't be known for their sartorial elegance. Also the jailer's daughter, Polly, would have had a simple dress. Leslie Harradine reproduced Lovat Fraser's designs very faithfully and the group proved very popular.

Polly Peachum was later adapted as Delight HN 1772 in 1936 and stayed in production until 1972

PAMELA HN 1469 1931

It was a very exciting find for me when I came across this cover from *Britania .& Eve* for September 1930. There was Pamela in every detail - a portrait of the Marchesa del Merito by the society painter of the day, Phillip de Laszlo. I once spoke to John Pierpoint, a retired figurine painter who worked in the 1930s and who remembered the incident, and he told me that a lawsuit was threatened because Pamela was such an obvious copy of the portrait.

The painter certainly had a strong case and he must have been a man full of his own importance. Philip de Laszlo was born in Budapest in 1869, the son of a Jewish tailor. He won a gold medal at the Paris Exhibition of 1900. He travelled to England in 1907 and became a British citizen in 1914. He painted Queen Alexandra and her husband Edward VII who awarded him the Royal Victorian Order. He painted Marina, Duchess of Kent, The Duchess of York, later Queen Elizabeth, the Mountbattens and our present Queen, aged 7 in 1933, her first ever portrait, together with the royals and aristocracy of Europe. He married into the wealthy Guinness family and his children and grandchildren married into the aristocracy. He died in 1937. I think this colourful character was the ultimate social climber!

Marina, Duchess of Kent and de Laszlo

PIERROT AND PIERRETTE 1924
Leslie Harradine

HN 642

The seaside concert party was a great entertainment in the1920s. The factories at Burslem closed down for wakes week and those who could afford it took excursion trains to Blackpool and other resorts.

The paid holiday was not instigated until 1934. It was a hard life in the Potteries in previous times with the only time off being on Saturday afternoon and Sunday with very few other wakes days. These were at first related to holy days, but later developed into local celebrations with a fair and sports competitions. The workers of the 1920s would have been familiar with the pierrot entertainers if only from their use in the advertising of everything from boot polish to Tom Smith's Christmas crackers. Tom Smith was the first to put the crack in crackers.

DREAMLAND HN1473 1931 Leslie Harradine

Dreamland was a musical comedy of 1921. It was about a girl who fell in love with a pierrot making it so obviously the inspiration for this model.

The 1920s and 1930s were the age of the pierrot. In 1923 Gertrude Lawrence sang *Parisian Pierrot* in Noël Coward's review *London Calling.* J B Priestly wrote a popular book about a pierrot concert party called *The Good Companions* which was made into a film at Lime Grove Studios, Shepherd's Bush, London in 1932 with John Gielgud as the romantic lead. *The Co-Optimists,* a stage variety revue opened at the Royalty Theatre in 1921 and ran until 1926. It was an all-star pierrot entertainment which ran for 500 performances.

THE MASKED BALL

Most of this group of characters created by Leslie Harradine have an association with the masked ball much loved at the time. These attractive ladies appeared in many colourways. They are very popular with collectors today and command higher and higher prices in the salerooms.

Folly HN 1750 1936, The Mask HN 657 1924 and Lady Jester HN 1285 1928 are shown here and there are others such as Clownette HN 717 1925 and Harlequinade HN 585 1923.

BUTTERFLY HN 719 1925

MEPHISTO HN 723 1925

MARIETTA HN 1341 1929

Harradine took much inspiration for this type of figure from the theatre. Here is the ballerina Adeline Genée in her costume for *A Dream of Butterflies and Roses* at the London Coliseum in 1915. The French Alice Delysia, after her debut at the Moulin Rouge in Paris, returned to London and became a star overnight in *Odds & Ends* in 1914. In a Cochran Revue of 1925 *On With the Dance* she became one of Noël Coward's leading ladies and sang his memorable song *Poor Little Rich Girl.* She appears as *Lucifer* in the costume shown here, which image became the inspiration behind one of Doulton's most popular figurines, Marietta. In the Second World War Alice Delysia entertained the troops in the desert.

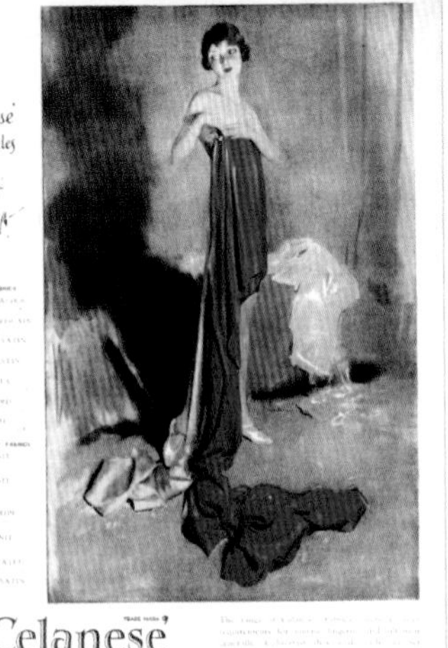

NEGLIGÉE HN 1219 1927 AND CELIA HN 1726 1935
Leslie Harradine

These Celanese adverts by H C Oliver, appearing in copies of *Woman's Journal* and *Britannia & Eve* in 1927 and 1928, were certainly the inspiration behind Negligée and Celia. Leslie Harradine also adapted Elfreda HN 2078 1951 from another Celanese illustration taken from the March 1948 edition of *Country Life.*

Celanese was an early man-made fabric first made in England in 1918 by a Swiss inventor, Camille Dreyfus. It was advertised as 'artificial silk'.

LIDO LADY HN 1299 1927
Leslie Harradine

The Lido in Venice was the most fashionable bathing place in Europe at the time, a place to see and be seen. Noël Coward sang a song satirising lido fashions of which a pyjama style costume was one. This was another Oliver illustration for a Celanese advertisement in *Britannia & Eve.* In the 1920s and 1930s many towns in England had their lido consisting of an outdoor swimming pool complex.

SUNSHINE GIRL HN 1348 1929 Leslie Harradine

The Sunshine Girl, a musical play, was first performed at the Gaiety Theatre in 1912. It starred one of the pin-ups of the day, Phyllis Dare, who appeared in a swimming costume. The play introduced the tango to British audiences. The story revolved around a love affair between a factory girl and the owner.

The setting was very obviously based on the Port Sunlight Factory near Liverpool. Lord Lever, a philanthropist, set up his factory making Sunlight and Pear's soap on the Wirral in 1888. He also built there a model village complete with a theatre, a concert hall, an art gallery, a church, a school, a cottage hospital, a public house, *The Bridge Inn,* and a swimming pool for his workers. There are 900 Grade II listed buildings there today and it is being considered as a World Heritage Site.

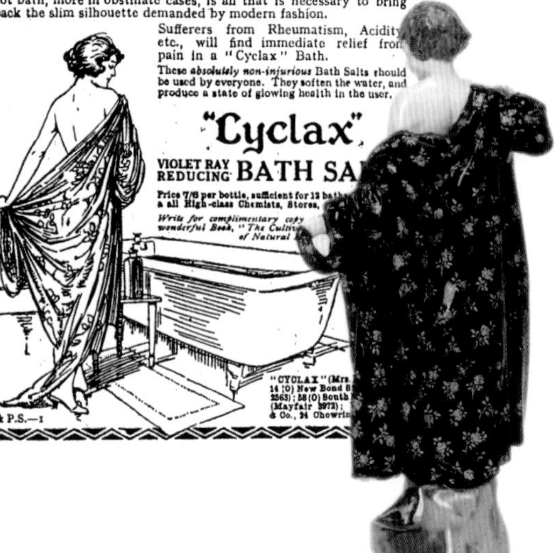

HN 1238

HN 687

THE BATHER HN 597 1924
Leslie Harradine

This is the advertisement for Cyclax bath salts which appeared in Mrs Harradine's copy of *Good Housekeeping* in 1924 when it caught her husband's attention, for again it is a direct copy.

In 1935 a bathing costume was added to this model as HN 1708. Skirt lengths went down to the ankles for afternoon wear at this time; there was a cover-up after the skimpy dresses and nudity of the 1920s.

DORCAS HN 1558 1933
Leslie Harradine

Dorcas is a biblical character who helped the poor. She is usually associated with seamstresses and laundresses, hence this advertisement for Dorcas towels in *Britannia & Eve* of April 1930 which may have given this idea to Harradine.

MISS 1926, HN 1205 1926 Leslie Harradine

Many of Harradine's models were based on the fashions of the time. Here is a Swears & Wells advert in a *Britannia & Eve* of 1929.

Courtesy Charlton Collection.

Rhapsody in Blue - - - - -

DAYDREAMS HN 1732 1935 AND SWEETING HN 1935 1940
Leslie Harradine

Harradine took these two figures direct from magazine adverts for Marshall & Snellgrove, 'Garment and Textile Retailers of Distinction in London for over 100 years', who built their own store at 334-348 Oxford Street in 1851. They cultivated an air of exclusivity with their own couture workroom. It cost 60 guineas to enrol in the workrooms as an apprentice. Closed in the 1960s it became Debenhams's in 1973.

HUNTS LADY HN 1201 1926
Leslie Harradine

A very smart hunter as featured in adverts by Moss Bros and Harry Hall. There was a companion The Huntsman HN 1226 1927.

Courtesy Photo Express

THE PRINCE OF WALES
HN 1217 1926
Leslie Harradine

Edward, the eldest son of George V and heir to the throne was invested as Prince of Wales in 1911. He was a popular social figure. He succeeded to the throne in 1936 for a short reign from January to December of that year when he abdicated in order 'to marry the woman I love.'

Wallis Simpson was an American divorcee and not considered a suitable consort for the Defender of the Faith by the 'establishment'. He was exiled but remained popular with the people.

He was a keen horseman as the figure suggests, where he appears dressed as he was in this painting by Sir Alfred Munnings. He received the following advice from his father as a young man; 'If you can't ride well, I'm afraid people will think you a duffer.'

THE SKETCH GIRL 1923 Leslie Harradine

This figure was commissioned by *The Sketch* magazine and consequently has no HN number. 'Miss Sketch' appeared on the front of the magazine and this is a very faithful copy of her by Doulton. In her tray she carries mini figures representing the subjects covered by the publication, the ballerina for the theatre, the jockey for sport, the cupid for romance, the soldier for current affairs and the devil represents satire.

The Sketch in 1927 presented the figurine as a prize to the winner of their crossword puzzle.

There was also a Sketch cat designed by George Studdy, here attending a fancy dress ball at his debut in 1909. Ooloo later became the Doulton animal figure, Lucky K 12.

MAM'SELLE HN 658 1924
Leslie Harradine

The Vanity Girl, by Compton Mackenzie, 'a romance of the stage', appeared in the *The Story-Teller* of 1919. Here Harradine features an earlier fashion.

THE PERFECT PAIR HN 581 1923
Leslie Harradine

Here is a commissioned group representing the amalgamation of two magazines *Eve,* a ladies pictorial and *The Tatler* in 1923. The red coated gentleman always appeared on the cover of *The Tatler,* a society chat magazine. This 1923 advert is by the illustrator Mabel Lucie Atwell.

STANDING BEEFEATER 1924

This figure was commissioned by *The Illustrated London News* which was a current affairs magazine first published in 1842. It used woodcuts and engravings and later photography as illustrations on a large scale, sending artists worldwide to record the news. It was published weekly at first but became monthly in 1971 and in the 21st century is still published twice a year. The figure holds a miniature facsimile of the first edition of the paper.

Beefeaters perform as the Queen's bodyguard on state occasions. They often today double as Yeomen Warders of the Tower of London where they are often erroneously labelled.

YARDLEY'S LAVENDER

This group is a straight adaptation of Yardley's advertising group which in turn was adapted from Wheatley's *Cries of London.* Reco Capey, who was born and studied in Burslem and did designs for both the Burslem and Lambeth Doulton factories, was art director at Yardley's at the time and probably instituted this figure. Later on we show how Leslie Harradine adapted elements from Wheatley's *Cries of London* so that he was very probably the modeller in this instance too.

TSANG IHANG HN 582 1923

This advertisement for Grossmith's Tsang Ihang Perfume of Thibet showing this figure has eluded me for thirty years only to be found very recently by Christopher Evans. It makes a very different figurine, and although the modeller is not given it does have an HN number. Nevertheless it was probably not for general issue but only used in stores as a promotional display piece.

NELL GWYNNE HN 1882 1938

This image Harradine took from a Player's cigarette card in the series *Famous Beauties.* My father smoked this brand in the 1930s and I collected the cards. The card shows Nell with her basket of oranges which she sold to the audience at the Drury Lane theatre. She attracted the attention of the King when he attended a performance there and she became his mistress in 1669. King Charles II was known as the Merry Monarch and had many mistresses but Nell seemed to be the favourite. She bore him two sons. On his death bed Charles is recorded as saying, 'let not poor Nellie starve'. She influenced the founding of the Royal Hospital at Chelsea as a home for old soldiers which still exists today. Leslie Harradine had modelled a Chelsea Pensioner HN 689 in 1924 in his distinctive red uniform.

A film with Anna Neagle taking the part of Nell Gywnne was shown in 1934 which may have prompted the choice of this subject.

LUCY ANN HN1502 1932 Leslie Harradine

This was taken from a charming portrait of a Miss Murray by Sir Thomas Lawrence.1769-1830.

HN 1565 1938

ANTOINETTE HN1850 1938

Leslie Harradine

Another figure inspired by a card from Player's *Famous Beauties* series was of Marie Antoinette. A film with Norma Shearer in the starring role as Marie Antoinette partnered by Tyrone Power was released in 1938. She was a tragic figure, in that Marie Antoinette, Queen to Louis XVI was a victim of the French Revolution and guillotined in 1793.

HOLLYWOOD GLAMOUR OF THE 1930s AND 1940s

Harradine modelled some very glamorous figures from time to time which, although they are not attributable to a particular Hollywood production, are the epitome of many of them. The sleek lines with their bias cuts and satin finishes are mirrored in Clotilde HN 1598 1933, The Mirror HN 1852 1938, Rhythm HN 1903 1939 and Collinette HN 1998 1947.

STEVE 1926-36 6.5"

Made for Wettern, Beadle & Bristow, road builders and asphalt suppliers. One of their directors told me that Steve actually existed and the model was a caricature of their foreman of that name. It would be good to see a photograph of the original.

On the base is the inscription 'mend your ways and consult Steve' but copies exist without this addition.

THE DAILY TELEGRAPH, MONDAY, JANUARY 14, 1918

The SENTINEL
STEAM WAGGON

Saves over 30/- a day on your haulage fuel bill and reduces repair expenses to a minimum.

The proof for the asking.

Alley & MacLellan
Ltd.
SHREWSBURY.

SENTINEL
THE ECONOMICAL STEAM WAGGON

THE SENTINEL HN 523 1921 17.5"

The Sentinel Waggon Works, makers of locomotives, steam lorries and other vehicles, commissioned this piece. The Sentinel was their logo and appeared on the entrance gates of their factory. His shield carries the Arms of Shrewsbury where the works were situated and the motto, 'Ever Watchful and on the Alert'. The firm later became Rolls Royce.

Courtesy Whitley Collection

TOWN CRIER HN 2119 1953
Peggy Davies

HN 2108

Harradine, as we have seen, liked to work from illustrations. Peggy Davies on the other hand often worked from life. The Master HN 2325 she based on her father. She used her husband, Sylvan, as the original for the Town Crier. He stood with his mouth open for hours and when he was at last allowed to smoke she grabbed his pipe at one point and pressed the mouthpiece into the clay to simulate the embroidery on his waistcoat. His arm must have ached if he had to appear to be ringing a bell for long. She used her small son Rhodri in his fancy dress suit for Baby Bunting HN 2108 1953. She used Rhodri as a model later in The One that Got Away HN 2153 1955.

She had two other sons Gethin and Sylvan and used them for, River Boy HN 2128 1962 and Treasure Island HN 2243 1962.

THE LEISURE HOUR HN 2055 1950
Peggy Davies

This name is taken from the title of a ladies magazine published in the 1880s whose pages were full of stories and pastimes. The model shows a lady from the 17th century reading. I'm not sure if there was anything as frivolous as ladies leisure reading then but it couldn't all have been religious and Latin texts.

Peggy was particularly interested in historical costume.

THE FOAMING QUART HN 2162 1955
Peggy Davies

Here Peggy has used a photograph of the famous actor-manager, Sir Herbert Beerbohm Tree, 1872-1956 in the role of Falstaff from *The Merry Wives of Windsor.* He built Her Majesty's Theatre and was knighted in 1909.

KATE GREENAWAY 1846-1901

KATE GREENAWAY'S FAMILY TREASURY

Selections from Kate Greenaway's A Applepie, Book of Games, Marigold Garden, Mother Goose, and Under the Window

HN 2833 Sophie

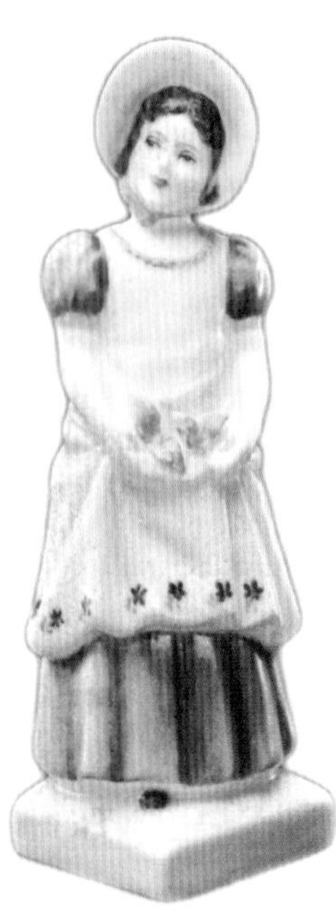

HN 2834 Emma

Kate Greenaway illustrated children's books and her first one *Under the Window* published in 1878 sold 20,000 copies immediately and created the Greenaway style. The children wore a Regency revival type of dress and there were sunflowers and lilies redolent of the 1880's aesthetic fashion. The gardens had a Bedford Park air which was a recently built garden suburb in London which became an artists' community.

Peggy Davies showed her versatility in that she seemed to be able to represent children, characters, animals, and historical subjects as well as the ladies which were regarded as her main speciality.

Peggy did eleven Greenaway children from 1976-1978. The series was so successful that Doulton continued the set later using Pauline Parsons.

INDIAN BRAVE HN 2376 1967
Peggy Davies

In seeking a model for this Prestige piece she went to a youth club which was run by her husband. When the boys were paraded before her she picked out the scrawniest of them much to the pride of the model and the chagrin of the rest, but Peggy explained to them that there was no fat on a Plains Indian. His mount was a local Police horse.

MATADOR AND BULL
HN 2324 1964 Peggy Davies

Peggy studied the bulls at the Artificial Insemination Centre at Teen in Staffordshire and an abattoir for this model.

THE PALIO HN 2428 1971

Peggy Davies

Peggy travelled to Sienna, Italy to research this figure at the famous horse race.

THE FESTIVAL OF BRITAIN 1951

HN 2191 HN 2192

This festival celebrated the end of the dark days of World War II. Food rationing was almost at an end and there was a great interest in the future. A site was cleared in the bomb damage on the South Bank of the Thames in central London. Our top architects created large impressive buildings to house the best our designers could present for a new world for all. Doulton was well represented and many Lambeth and Burslem artists exhibited their work. Doulton Lambeth brought colour to the site by providing 60 large Ali Baba jars as flower containers. There was music and open-air space for dancing and an air of celebration, but as it celebrated the centennial of the Great Exhibition of 1851 in Hyde Park it was also a showcase for the best that Britain could produce. A definite style developed which was of the time and Peggy Davies with Jo Ledger, art director, did a series of figurines which epitomised it with their clean elongated lines. There was a feeling of new beginnings and a youth-oriented spirit begun which coloured the 1950s and 1960s. This range of figures represented that: Sweet Sixteen HN2231 with a ponytail - very fashionable then. Others were Columbine HN 2185, Harlequin HN 2186, Sea Sprite HN 2191, Wood Nymph HN 2192, Melody HN 2202 and Teenager HN 2203.

The contemporary elongated figure was exhibited by sculptress Daphne Hardy.

THE INTERNATIONAL EXPOSITION, BRUSSELS 1958

Peggy Davies created her prize-winning figure *The Marriage of Art and Industry* HN 2261 especially for this occasion which Price Phillip, whilst visiting the Doulton stand, re-christened *'Young Love in Brussels'.* He also made one of his usual quips to Desmond Eyles about the comfort of the loos at Buckingham Palace and couldn't Doulton do something better? 12 copies of the group were made but not for resale.

BALLERINA HN 2116 1953 Peggy Davies

A Ballerina with red shoes? This can only mean she is taken from the film, *The Red Shoes* by Powell and Pressburger, released in 1948. The ballerina was played by Moira Shearer, a leading dancer of the time who had red hair as the figure has and danced in this very beautiful film. It told of a girl who became a great star but commits suicide when torn between love and her career. There must have been some consultation between Peggy and the marketing board here as the modeller didn't usually have any say in the colours used. Moira Shearer was 22 at this time. She later gave up classical ballet for acting.

GYPSY DANCE HN 2230 1959 Peggy Davies

A dancer with bare feet? This has to be from the film *The Barefoot Contessa* 1954 where Ava Gardner played a Spanish gipsy girl who became a great Hollywood star but betrayed her roots by preferring to dance in bare feet.

There is a version with hand extended. Figures were often adapted at a later date if the pose was liable to breakages because of its construction.

PIROUETTE HN 2216 1959 Peggy Davies

Ash blonde hair, a halter neckline and a swirling skirt as worn by Marilyn Monroe in the film of 1955, *The Seven Year Itch.*

The skirt is longer than the famous original which blew up over the grating as skirts have to support a figure. In every case Peggy had no say in the name but with a character taken from a US film there is always a risk of copyright difficulties if the original name is used.

EASTER DAY HN 1976 1945 Leslie Harradine

Back to Harradine showing again his habit of copying - in this case a photograph - in every detail. This is Vivien Leigh as Scarlet O'Hara in that great epic of 1938, *Gone With the Wind**, translated into a demure miss. In 1999 Doulton issued Scarlet O'Hara HN 4200 by Valerie Annand and you could not display these two figures next to one another: the fact it was only in production for a year says all.

MARY NICOLL 1922-1974

Mary's father was Gordon Nicoll who had illustrated some Doulton Lambeth publications and who recommended his daughter to Desmond Eyles, who in turn recommended her to Jack Noke at Burslem.

She produced many character figures for the range; they were full of personality and humanity. Many of them were inspired by the fishermen and characters who lived in her Devon town and appeared as Sea Harvest HN 2257 1969, Helmsman HN 2499 1974, and The Lobster Man HN 2323 1987. She worked as a freelance for Doulton for twenty five years until her untimely death.

TUPPENCE A BAG HN 2320 1968
Mary Nicoll

This character is inspired by the Disney film *Mary Poppins* released in 1964. It featured an old lady who sold bird seed from the steps of St Paul's Cathedral. The film in turn was based on a series of children's books by P L Travers. Mary Nicoll was particularly good at representing the older generation.

THE DETECTIVE HN 2359 1977 Mary Nicoll

Mary Nicoll was also good at male characters. Her detective is obviously a portrayal of Basil Rathbone as Sherlock Holmes in a series of a dozen films made between 1939 and 1946 in Hollywood when escapist stories were needed in troubled times. The fictional character was first created by Sir Arthur Conan Doyle in *A Study in Scarlet* in 1887 and has had a great following ever since.

BILL HARPER

Born in the Potteries in 1923, Bill has studied and worked there all his life but has travelled to some of the remoter parts of the world at times. His first journey was as a result of World War II when he joined the R.A.F. in 1942 as a wireless operator/air gunner. In 1944, when things were a little more peaceful, he found himself between duties taking life drawing classes in the Royal Palace in Naples, Italy. Here he had discovered his *forte.*

When he returned to the Potteries at the age of 22 he made a new start and enrolled at the Burslem School of Art to study painting and pottery. He joined the Wade company as a designer in 1954 and rose to become head designer and a junior director. Leaving Wade in 1962 he set up his own Mayflower Pottery in Tunstall designing and modelling a range of animal models. He became a designer for W H Bossons and modelled many of their masks until 1971. It was in 1972 that he first began modelling for Doulton on a freelance basis, a contract which lasted for almost 30 years until 2000. During that time he meticulously researched, designed, and modelled figurines in every category; character studies, ladies and children. He also produced character jug models in all sizes but specialising in 'Tinies' which required minute detail. His own range of *Doultonville* toby jugs were a popular success and he was responsible for so much more from the Diamond collection to a range of character teapots. He was referred to as the 'backbone of the company'.

In the earlier years he designed about 20 figures a year which went on pilot surveys to the United States stores. Only 5 or 6 might be chosen by the collectors and the remainder, with all the research and work they represented, were shelved. These are the prototypes which the company have sold in the auction rooms recently and for which the collectors pay thousands of pounds. Very many of them were Bill's. The money they attain would have been very useful in educating his three children in earlier days. Bill mourns the demise of the Doulton Company and the way their talents have become unappreciated.

However, his retirement became a new beginning for all his many interests. He enrolled as a student at his local university and began a writing career. He studies philosophy, writes poetry, and has produced books and dissertations which have reached world - wide distribution and fame. Bill has attended Doulton events all over the world and is popular with his collectors for his modest and gentle disposition and respected for his talent, knowledge and courteous manner. In his spare time he has climbed the mountains of the world including the Himalayas, the Andes and the Tien Shan. He now walks in the Peak district near his home.

THANKS DOC HN 2731 1975 Bill Harper

Bill used his border collie 'Laddie' as a model for this group and the vet looks rather like Bill.

VOTES FOR WOMEN HN 2816 1978 Bill Harper

In New Zealand women achieved the vote in 1893. In the UK it was not until 1928. The Suffragettes campaigned vigorously and violently for their vote from the early 1900s. They suffered prison sentences and even death in their efforts for their cause but it was their very active part in the First World War which did most to gain them equality.

Here Bill has taken inspiration from a famous poster of the time. The green, violet and white of the sash represent the initial letters of their demand 'Give Votes to Women'.

VOTES FOR WOMEN
1D
VOTES FOR WOMEN
VOTES
FOR
WOMEN
H.M. Dallas
HERE!

LORD OLIVIER AS RICHARD III HN 2881 1985 Eric Griffiths

Eric Griffiths was able to get some help from life as he met Lord Olivier prior to his sculpting this figure.

Doulton had always drawn on freelance artists for their figurine designs but in 1972 they set up their own in-house studio with Eric Griffiths as Director of Sculpture. Peter Gee and Robert Tabbenor joined him as trainee modellers in 1972. The design studio existed until 1990 when Eric Griffiths left. Peter Gee and Robert Tabbenor became freelance artists - the latter does models for the Moorcroft factory amongst others. Eric Griffiths spoke of 'my 20 happy years with Doulton.'

THE AUCTIONEER HN 2988
1986 Robert Tabbenor

This was a Royal Doulton International Collectors Club issue and the subject was suggested by Louise Irvine, the club director. It bears some resemblance to a popular auctioneer, Eric Knowles, in that he sported a moustache and wore a characteristic bow tie at the rostrum. He is one of the stars of the BBC's *Antiques Road Show.* However, Robert says he based the face on the actor Ronnie Barker. Eric Griffiths encouraged them to search magazines for suitable faces and Robert once based a pose for a figure on one he found of Bianca Jagger and one of the Flambé eastern figures he did was taken from an Arthur Rackham illustration.

He did two other very good models for RDICC issues, Prized Possessions HN 2942 and Pride and Joy HN 2945 which he modelled on Desmond Eyles, the Doulton historian. Another of his figures The China Repairer HN 2943 was of a Mr Howard Hockridge, a china repairer from Toronto, Canada and the figure was pre-released there in 1982.

HN 2945

HN 2943

ELIZA HN 2543 1974 Eric Griffiths 12"

Eric Griffiths created this figure as part of the *Haute Ensemble* series. The elongated style suited the subject of Eliza from *My Fair Lady* which had been very popular since its appearance in 1956. Lerner & Lowe adapted the musical from George Bernard Shaw's play *Pygmalion.* Its leads were Rex Harrison and Julie Andrews. When a film was made in Hollywood in 1964 Rex kept his part but Audrey Hepburn played Eliza.

KATE HANNIGAN HN 3088
1989 Eric Griffiths

Catherine Cookson with Eric Griffiths

The author Dame Catherine Cookson OBE, 1906-1998, took a personal interest in the production of this figure. Kate Hannigan was the title of the first of her popular novels which was published in 1947 when she was aged 40. She went on to publish 100 books in all which were translated into 20 languages. Sales eventually reached 123,000,000 in her lifetime alone. She wrote of the times and places she was familiar with in the North of England.

This is the first time Doulton reproduced a character created by a living author. Eric Griffiths travelled to her home in Northumberland so that the 80 year old authoress could study the sketches and approve the original clay model. Speaking of the model she said, 'I am honoured that my character is being produced in this way. Kate Hannigan had a hard life but she was a soft, warm character. The shape of her head is lovely, also the curve of her back, beautiful, just as I see her. I wondered how she would look. This is marvellous and I am delighted. I love her.'

The tradition of copying models from famous paintings continued into the 1990's with issues such as:

GAINSBOROUGH COLLECTION - one of which is
MARY, COUNTESS OF HOWE
HN 3007 1990 Peter Gee

REYNOLDS COLLECTION - one of which is
LADY WORSLEY HN 3318 1991 Peter Gee

JAMES TISSOT 1836 -1902

L'AMBITIEUSE HN 3359 1991

Valerie Annand

Tissot was a French painter of elegant society, especially women. He came to London from 1872 to 1892 and painted the *demi monde* and scenes of the Thames.

Here follow a very significant number of influences, researched by Christopher Evans, which were used by Doulton's modellers in the range. They show clearly how much they were influenced by other artists' work, both painters and illustrators. In a very few instances Doulton purchased the use of the image, but in most cases they were purloined from illustrations, some created originally for calendars and greeting cards. Many have been adapted, others are straight copies. The greatest exponent was, of course, Leslie Harradine. The search continues . . .

RAPHAEL TUCK

To all Doulton figure collectors the name Raphael Tuck is synonymous with the origins of some of the archetypal Doulton figures of the late 1930s. For what is now considered a relatively small fee, Doulton purchased the 'sole rights to reproduction in china' of a handful of Tuck images, some of which went on to become Doulton's most successful figures ever, with several even re-emerging into the current Doulton catalogue for 2009. As well as Tuck we can also add the name of Valentine, another publisher of the early twentieth century.

STANISLAUS SOUTTEN LONGLEY 1894 - 1966

Longley was a watercolour landscape and decorative figure painter and enjoyed a long and successful career, even producing posters for the London Underground group, commissioned in the 1920s. During World War II he served as a camouflage officer where his artistic talents were put to use recording daily army life. His later pictures are of seascapes and idyllic sea-side scenes, which coincided with his move to the south coast of England.

In the Royal Doulton International Collector's Club magazine (Vol. 3 No. 2) they recounted the story of an impoverished Longley approaching Doulton to ask whether they could forward him any examples of his figures, one particular figure mentioned being The Cherry Harvest, a girl sitting on a wall with a basket of cherries. Although never put into production, here is the original Longley picture. This particular picture was exhibited at the Royal Society of British Artists in 1932 and found again on the Valentine calendar.

I was once lucky enough to see a Tuck sample book containing many instantly recognisable images.

All these by Leslie Harradine.

Untitled - LADY APRIL HN 1965 1941

***Unexpected Meeting* -**

LADY CHARMIAN

HN 1948 1940

These figures were also taken from Longley originals:

CAMILLE HN 1586
HONEY HN 1909
AUTUMN BREEZES HN 1911
ROSEANNA HN 1921
MERIEL HN 1932
MARGUERITE HN 1928
HER LADYSHIP HN 1977
CHRISTMAS MORN HN 1992

All by Leslie Harradine except the last entry by Peggy Davies.

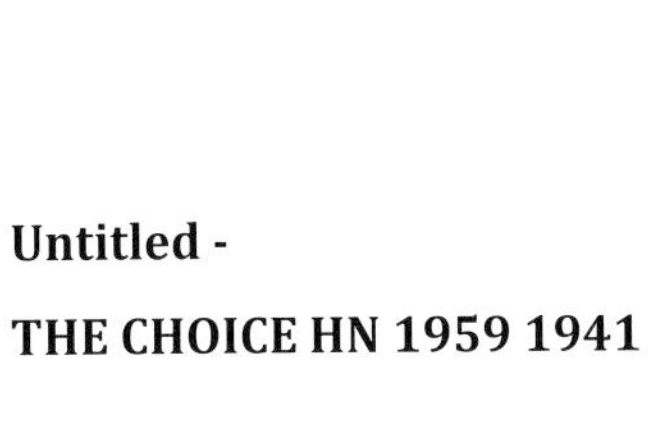

Untitled -

THE CHOICE HN 1959 1941

A Lady of Fashion - **GENEVIEVE**

HN 1962 1941

It became clear that Doulton often held on to Harradine's models for several years, as I found the picture for Top o'the Hill HN 1834 executed for Tuck by Molly Benatar in 1937 alongside one by Longley for Bedtime Story HN 2059 which was not introduced until 1950.

TOP O' THE HILL HN 1834 1937

MOLLY BENATAR

Molly Benatar worked largely as an illustrator and particularly as a children's book illustrator with her illustrations appearing in many titles from the 1920s onwards. Her first work for Tuck for which Doulton purchased the reproduction rights was Top o'the Hill, which was purchased for the princely sum of 5 guineas in 1937. Doulton apparently objected to the price and thanks to Tuck lowering the prices of other Benatar pictures to 4 guineas, you can see a selection of other figures inspired by her.

As with all Doulton records, preserving them seems to have been a problem. Thus it is always with an open mind that the search for material continues. It was in this way that I happened across this Benatar picture produced by Raphael Tuck, simulating a mother of pearl finish to the original illustration. Here we clearly have Harradine's Sweet and Twenty HN1298 1928 under the title 'When Hearts Were Young'. The Doulton title for this figure came from the song *O Mistress Mine* in Shakespeare's *Twelfth Night;*

'Then come kiss me, sweet-and-twenty,
Youth's a stuff will not endure.'

When Hearts were Young -
SWEET & TWENTY
HN 1649 1934

Call of the Winds - **SPRING MORNING HN 1922 1940**

The Bluebird's Message -

LYDIA HN 1906 1939

MISS MUFFET HN 1936 was also taken from a Benatar original.

All again by Leslie Harradine.

The Robin's Message -
TOINTETTE
HN 1940
1940

Tulip Time -
SWEET SUZY HN 1918 1939

ARTHUR GARRATT 1873 - 1955

With works in national collections in UK, you might expect to find more pictures of his here; however, to date there are just two. The first is Aileen HN1664 1934 and *A Sweetheart of Mine.* The second is Rosabell HN1620 1934 and *Alice Blue Gown*, the title coming from two separate sources; firstly the popular song of that name and secondly from Alice Roosevelt Longworth, daughter of the former American President. This second link is not only in the title and the dress in the picture being in Longworth's signature colour, but the picture also bears a strong resemblance to Longworth. Her exploits earned her the title 'Alice in Plunderland' during a trip to Asia and, interestingly, she would also wear a costly string of pearls, a gift from the Cuban government, for the rest of her life. Many of Garratt's pictures feature a young lady sporting a shawl; an image which Doulton, too, seem to have favoured during the early twentieth century.

Both figures are by Leslie Harradine.

ANNE ROCHESTER

Only one illustration by this artist appears to have been incorporated into the range and this was from the publisher Valentine. The illustration, being titled *The Seamstress,* was used again, by Harradine, for Penelope HN 1901 1939.

It was re-named by Doulton, although the reference to Penelope keeps the theme alive as Penelope, wife of Ulysses, kept her suitors at bay by undoing all the embroidery she had done by day, whilst waiting for her husband to return from his adventures. The name Penelope was also used by one tapestry manufacturer of the period, the relevance not being wasted. As an artist Rochester, too, is credited with illustrating many children's stories from the 1920s and 1930s.

LANCELOT ROBERTS
1883 - 1950

Roberts originated from Derbyshire, lived in the Midlands and later moved to Egglesbach, North Wales with his wife. He had a long and commercially successful career, although only one of his pictures was exhibited in London. In addition to his picture *Springtime* for Tuck he also painted portraits and landscapes. I have seen several other calendar illustrations of his and they appear in much the same romantic vein. Harradine modelled Springtime HN 1971 1941 from Roberts' painting.

JENNIE HARBOUR

Jennie Harbour is now seen as one of the great children's fairy tale book and postcard illustrators of the Art Deco era. Very little is known about the artist though her work is in considerable demand today. Much of her work was published by Raphael Tuck

***Pretty to Walk With* -**
ANNABELLA
HN 1871 1938

***The Peacocks* -**
MODENA
HN 1846 1938

although I have also come across one of her pictures adorning a powder puff, which I found in the USA.

These figures were also taken from Harbour originals:

LADY & BLACKAMOOR HN 374
CARMEN HN 1267
SPANISH LADY HN 1262
PAISLEY SHAWL HN 1392
PHYLLIS HN 1420
BARBARA HN 1421
TILDY HN 1576
SIBELL HN 1695
MILADY HN 1970
PRUE HN 1996

My Ladye -

LADY CLARE HN 1465 1931

A Rosy Ruse -

MISS FORTUNE HN 1898 1938

DION CLAYTON CALTHROP 1878-1937

Calthrop's influence on the HN range can only be described as great since so many of Doulton's artists appear to have used his illustrations as inspiration from the earliest times. The illustration shown here are all taken from his book *English Costume.*

A WOMAN OF THE TIME OF HENRY VI

HN 43 1914

Ernest Light

MARGARET OF ANJOU

HN 2012 1948

Peggy Davies

SIR THOMAS LOVELL HN 356 1919 Charles Noke

This continued through to 1948 with Peggy Davies and her period figures in the *English History* Range introduced in 1948.

ELEANOR OF PROVENCE

HN 2009 1948

Peggy Davies

WILLIAN POWELL FRITH 1819-1909

HN 1514

Harradine took this figure from a painting by Frith which was once owned by Charles Dickens and is now in the Victoria and Albert Museum. Dolly Varden is a character in Dickens' novel, Barnaby Rudge where he writes of her, *'... a face lighted up by the loveliest pair of sparkling eyes ... the face of a pretty, laughing, girl; dimpled and fresh, and healthful ... the very pink and pattern of good looks, in a smart little cherry-coloured mantle ... a little straw hat (and) she wore a cruel little muff'.*

Dickens created her as spoilt, vain and coquettish - a tipped-forward hat of this type is known as a 'Dolly Varden'.

CICELY MARY BARKER 1895-1973

The popular fairy illustrator can also be credited with influencing at least two of Harradine's fairies for the HN range Fairy HN1375 (third version) 1930 and Fairy HN1396 (fourth version) 1930.

She is widely popular today still and her fairies appear in many children's books.

HN 1375

HN 1396

FRANCIS WHEATLEY 1747 - 1801

Wheatley's *Cries of London* series is instantly recognised the world over and his link to the Doulton HN range is clear immediately when we see titles for figures such as London Cry, Strawberries HN 749 and London Cry, Turnips and Carrots HN 752 both issued in 1925. However, there is another figure that I only recently realised must be credited to another of Wheatley's pictures *Do you want any Matches?;* the clear difference in the Doulton figure being that she, Spring Flowers HN 1945 from 1940, is now a flower seller. Again, these three figures are all by Harradine. We must also remember that the original for the Yardley's advertisement was also a Wheatley cry titled *'Two bunches a penny Primroses, two bunches a penny.'*

ARTHUR RACKHAM 1867 - 1939

An early influence to Noke in particular, was the popular Edwardian illustrator, Arthur Rackham, who was born on September 19, 1867, in London, England. He studied at the Lambeth School of Art and was elected to membership of The Royal Watercolour Society amongst other bodies. His work can be described as prolific, and books he illustrated included *Rip van Winkle* 1905, *Alice in Wonderland* 1907, and many other children's books and classics throughout the years until his death in 1939. His last work, for *The Wind in the Willows,* was published posthumously.

PRETTY LADY 1920
Harry Tittensor

EDMUND DULAC
1882 - 1953

The great illustrator, Edmund Dulac was born in France in 1882. In 1904 he left for London and the start of a meteoric career. Like Arthur Rackham, he had a strong influence in the early years of the HN range.

BLUE BEARD HN 410 1920 Ernest Light

A chance happening across Dulac's *Picture Book for the French Red Cross* 1915 led to the discoveries of Blue Beard HN 75 1917, Ernest Light, Mandarin HN84 1918, Charles Noke and Princess Badoura HN 2081 1952, Harry Tittensor. Plus a further illustration I came across.

ONE OF THE FORTY HN 417 1920 Harry Tittensor

HN 501 & HN 480

MARY YOUNG HUNTER
1872 - 1947

Mary Young Hunter belongs to the group of Edwardian Pre-Raphaelite painters who were something of a rediscovery in the late twentieth century. Born in New Zealand, she had a long and successful career, together with her husband, in the UK and later in the USA .

The Duke's High Dame -
THE LADY ANNE HN87
1918 Ernest Light

Her style is so very reflective of the tastes of the Edwardian period, as can be seen from other illustrations in this book, something which Doulton, too, followed when it came to painting figures.

FIGURE ADAPTATIONS

As all figure collectors know, during the design process prototypes followed by pilot figures are produced. However, once a figure has gone into production that does not mean that further adaptation and transformation is not possible nor can this be ruled out.

At no other time and to no other group of figures does this more aptly apply than to those of the 1920s and 1930s. With production dates for this period being so sketchy one can only attempt to draw conclusions as to the precise dates of withdrawal and sometimes even introduction.

This is of particular relevance to a group of figures which are clear adaptations of existing ones. Take for example Harradine's Sweet Maid HN 1504 of 1932 which became Millicent HN 1714 of 1935 or Helen HN 1509 of 1932 which became June HN 1690 in 1935. The scarcity of the former in both cases suggests that the latter may have replaced these earlier models. Then again, we have The Old Lavender Seller HN 1492 of 1932 and Primroses HN 1617of 1934. Clearly the old lady is the same in both figures with minor adaptation. Both figures were produced simultaneously, as were the Rustic Swain HN 1745 of 1935 and Midsummer Noon HN 1899 of 1939.

However this tendency to adapt existing figures can be traced back to the earliest times of the HN figure range. Consider Noke's reintroduction of the

HN 1504 HN 1714 HN 1572 HN 1947

Jesters he had produced earlier in Vellum and then Pretty Lady HN 69 of 1916 and The Parson's Daughter HN 337 of 1919.

Existing models were not only adapted but also changed size and were renamed, such as Biddy HN 1445 and Rita HN 1448 of 1931 or Doris Keane HN90 of 1918 and Rosamund HN 1497 of 1932. Polly Peachum HN 463 was changed quite a lot to become Delight HN 1772 in 1936.

In my experience the date of 'by 1949' is rarely the case; indeed 'by 1944' would be more accurate, with the exception of a handful of the most popular figures of the time. Figures like The Old Balloon Seller HN 1315, which was in production for almost seventy years from 1929-1998 and others such as Autumn Breezes HN 1934 and Top o'the Hill HN 1849 were exported to the USA throughout World War II as return cargo for the Lend Lease sent by them. The production of these few figures continued into 1944 and was resumed soon after the end of the war.

HN 1745

HN 1899

Charles Noke's range of figurines numbered 4000 in 2003. Many subjects have been repeated through the years. Rising labour costs have meant the splendour of the early colouring and modelling are not commercial today. For this reason we have concentrated here on the early history as we approach the centennial of his idea, but Charles Noke could never have visualized the success of his idea or realised the pleasure he created for collectors all over the world.

INDEX

Figures and HN numbers are in **bold**

Other books by Jocelyn Lukins

Doulton for the Collector

Collecting Royal Doulton Character Jugs

Collecting Doulton Animals

Collecting Doulton Kingsware

Doulton Lambeth Advertising Wares

Doulton Burslem Advertising Wares

Doulton Flambé Animals

For articles and sales reports on Doulton see

www.collectingdoulton.com

The Sketch